better together*

* This book is best read together, grownup and kid.

a **akidsco.com**

a kids
book
about

a kids book about CHOSEN FAMILY

by Madi Bourdon

A Kids Co.
Editor Emma Wolf
Designer Rick DeLucco
Creative Director Rick DeLucco
Studio Manager Kenya Feldes
Sales Director Melanie Wilkins
Head of Books Jennifer Goldstein
CEO and Founder Jelani Memory

DK
Delhi Technical Team Bimlesh Tiwary Pushpak Tyagi, Rakesh Kumar
Senior Production Editor Jennifer Murray
Senior Production Controller Louise Minihane
Senior Acquisitions Editor Katy Flint
Acquisitions Project Editor Sara Forster
Managing Art Editor Vicky Short
Managing Director, Licensing Mark Searle

First American edition, 2025
Published in the United States by DK Publishing, 1745 Broadway, 20th Floor,
New York, NY 10019

First published in Great Britain in 2025 by
Dorling Kindersley Limited, 20 Vauxhall Bridge Road, London SW1V 2SA
A Penguin Random House Company

The authorised representative in the EEA is
Dorling Kindersley Verlag GmbH. Arnulfstr. 124, 80636 Munich, Germany

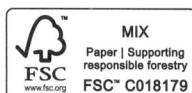

A catalog record for this book is available from the Library of Congress.
A CIP catalogue record for this book is available from the British Library.
ISBN: 978-0-2417-4367-6

DK books are available at special discounts when purchased in bulk for sales
promotions, premiums, fund-raising, or education use. For details, contact:
DK Publishing Special Markets, 1745 Broadway, 20th Floor, New York, NY 10019
SpecialSales@dk.com

Printed and bound in China
www.dk.com
akidsco.com

MIX
Paper | Supporting
responsible forestry
FSC™ C018179

This book was made with Forest
Stewardship Council™ certified
paper – one small step in DK's
commitment to a sustainable future.
**Learn more at www.dk.com/uk/
information/sustainability**

To all the given and chosen families around the world. Every human deserves as many people as possible who make them feel safe, loved, and celebrated for each and every part of themselves.

+ Kiara, Karissa, my GSA kids, and everyone I have chosen, who in turn have chosen me back.

Intro
for grownups

What is a chosen family? To me, chosen family are the people you invite into your heart who see (and love) you for your truest self. In communities all over the world, chosen family often plays a crucial role in providing emotional support, understanding, and unconditional love.

Chosen families can offer a unique alternative to traditional, biological families. But, this concept does not erase the importance of family in the traditional sense—they are not mutually exclusive. What I mean is, a chosen family is a group of souls who may not necessarily be related by shared DNA, but who choose to form deep, meaningful, and supportive connections with one another.

There is comfort in knowing there are people in our lives who recognize and value our uniqueness, and embrace our differences— no matter the relation.

Hey, Pals!

My name is Madi, and this is my book about **chosen family**.

Have you ever heard
of a "chosen family"?

It's kind of like the family you already know about, but it's also a little different.

You see, the term "chosen family" is pretty literal.

(Literal means something is exactly what it seems like it means.)

so, a chosen family is literally a family that you choose.

But, chosen family can
be a bit hard to define.

Mostly because chosen families can

be

different

for

everybody.

Many people have found chosen family outside of their biological family.

What is a **"biological family,"** you ask? Great question!

A biological family is the one you are born into. In other words, it's your given family.

Given family members often share special characteristics that make you, you.*

*But not *all* family members resemble each other!

Things like your hair color, your height, your eye color, and the color of your skin.

You might even share things like your favorite family recipes and traditions, or the similar ways your brain works.

Those are all special parts of you.

BUt there's way more that can make a family, a family.

Some people seek out and find their chosen family when their given family doesn't fully understand them or accept them for who they are.

Some people might need a different type of support than what their given family can provide, and that is OK.

My own chosen family is made up of people who accept and love me for my individuality.

My chosen family shares a love for things that mean a lot to me!

They understand...

how I express myself.

the things I need to feel whole.

what I need to feel like I belong.

My chosen family makes me feel OK about the things that make me different.

In fact, it's more than OK—my differences are celebrated!

And wanna know something really cool?

Chosen is totally

family unique!

My chosen family includes my students, the communities I identify with, people with shared experiences, my partner, and even my cousin!

I feel super lucky to have someone in my given family who is also in my chosen family.

Those people are extra special.

Who else can be in
your chosen family?

Your teammates.

Your coaches.

Your teachers.

Your neighbors.

Your pets.

Your friends at school.

Your counselor.

Your best friend's family.

And lots more!

Most importantly, chosen family are...

people who make
you feel safe,

people you trust,

people who make you feel
heard and understood,

and people who love you
for who you are now, *and*
who you are becoming.

It's important to know that chosen families aren't only created if someone's biological family is unsupportive.*

*If you are in a family situation that feels unsafe or harmful, please tell a trusted grownup.

The purpose of a chosen family can be to provide a different kind of support and validation than what you may find in your given family.

Have you ever heard the saying, "It's like comparing apples and oranges."?

Both apples and oranges are delish,
but they are completely different!

Family is kind of the same way!

Also, a chosen family isn't something you need to have.

You are whole and complete, just as you are.

Chosen family is about finding people who love, accept, and see you for you.

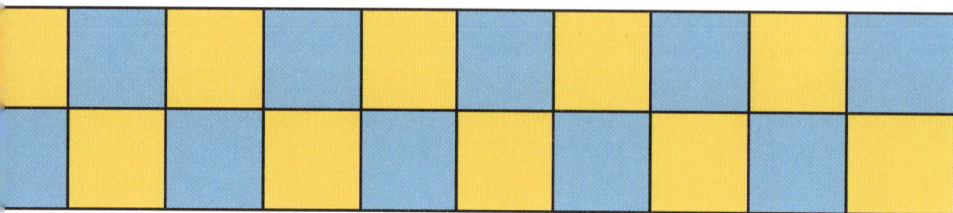

If you don't receive that from your given family, there are others who can give you that security.

If you do receive love and acceptance from your given family, that's special and awesome, too.

No matter who your given or chosen family is, it's all about how they make you feel, and that they allow you the freedom to be your truest self.

I found the people who make
me feel the most like me,
and you can too.

So, who makes you feel safest?

Who makes you feel the most comfortable in your skin?

Who makes you laugh the hardest?

Who motivates you?

Who makes you feel better when you're sad or hurt?

Who gives you
the best hugs?

Who can you be your silliest self with?

Who advocates for your needs?

Who can you tell your secrets to?

Who encourages you to feel pride in who you are?

Whoever you thought of when answering those questions,

those are your people.

Chosen or given,

they are the people who are family in the ways that matter.

Outro
for grownups

Whether chosen or given family, one is not more valuable than the other. This book is is an invitation to discuss the importance of finding your people—those who see and love you for you, biological or not.

Grownups, this is your chance to share a story about a time when you felt seen and supported by people outside of your given family. Who has supported your goals? Consistently shown up to offer a helping hand? Cared for you in tough times? Chosen families are a collection of friends, mentors, and allies who are there to celebrate achievements, provide guidance, and offer comfort. The concept of chosen family challenges traditional notions of family, demonstrating that strong, meaningful connections can be formed outside of biological relationships. This redefinition allows us to create bonds based on choice, rather than obligation.

So, to each and every person who has found or continues to create the bonds and connection every human needs—you are worthy of feeling seen, heard, and loved for who you truly are.

About The Author

Madi Bourdon (she/they) is a school counselor who believes collective care and connection is what powers our communities. Through this belief, she nurtures an atmosphere where students can create meaningful connections both within and beyond the school setting. Her commitment to empowering young people, especially in spaces where people can safely discover and embrace their authentic selves, is at the center of her work.

Madi wrote this book for her students, particularly those in her Gender and Sexuality Alliance (GSA) student group. Leading GSA allowed Madi to discover that chosen families come in many different forms. Whether they consist of 1 or 101 members, each holds a unique and significant role.

:camera: @madi_b_educating   :briefcase: @madi-bourdon

Made to empower.

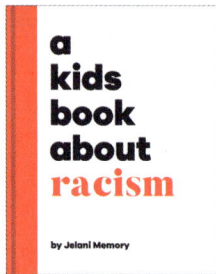

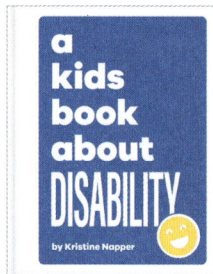

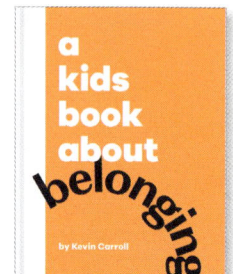

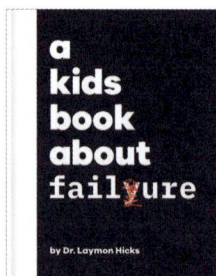

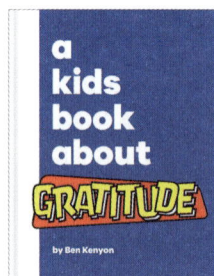

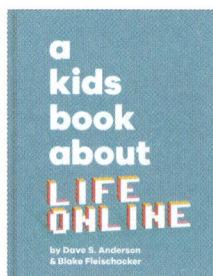

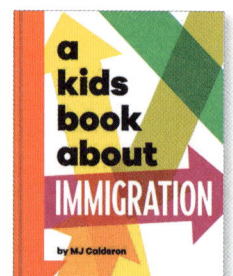

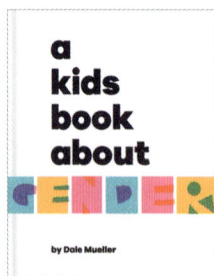

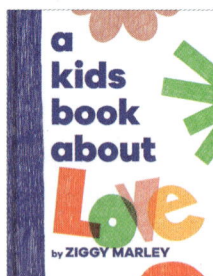

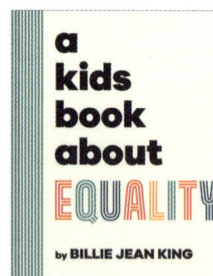

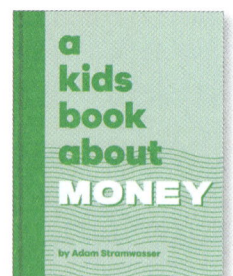

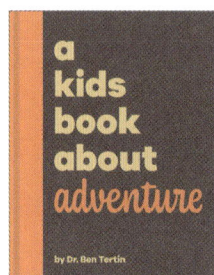

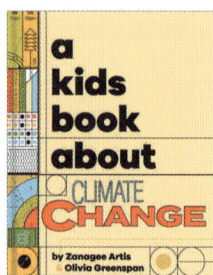

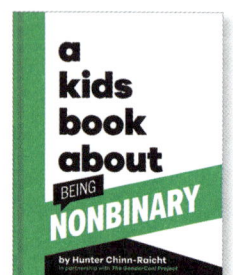

a kids book about **racism**
by Jelani Memory

a kids book about ANXIETY
by Ross Szabo

a kids book about DISABILITY
by Kristine Napper

a kids book about IMAGINATION
by LEVAR BURTON

a kids book about belonging
by Kevin Carroll

a kids book about failure
by Dr. Laymon Hicks

a kids book about GRATITUDE
by Ben Kenyon

a kids book about LIFE ONLINE
by Dave S. Anderson & Blake Fleischacker

a kids book about body image
by Rebecca Alexander

a kids book about IMMIGRATION
by MJ Calderon

a kids book about EMPATHY
by Daron K. Roberts

a kids book about GENDER
by Dale Mueller

a kids book about Love
by ZIGGY MARLEY

a kids book about EQUALITY
by BILLIE JEAN KING

a kids book about MONEY
by Adam Stramwasser

a kids book about FEMINISM
by Emma McIlroy

a kids book about adventure
by Dr. Ben Tertin

a kids book about CLIMATE CHANGE
by Zanagee Artis & Olivia Greenspan

a kids book about CONFIDENCE
by Joy Cho

a kids book about BEING NONBINARY
by Hunter Chinn-Raicht
in partnership with The GenderCool Project

Discover more at akidsco.com